A QUICK REFERENCE GUIDE TO THE END TIMES

JEFF KINLEY AND TODD HAMPSON

HARVEST HOUSE PUBLISHERS
EUGENE, OREGON

All Scripture quotations in chapters 2, 4, 5, and 6 are taken from the Holy Bible, New International Version®, NIV®. Copyright © 1973, 1978, 1984, 2011 by Biblica, Inc.® Used by permission. All rights reserved worldwide.

All Scripture quotations in chapters 1, 3, 7, 8, 9, and 10 are taken from the New American Standard Bible®, © 1960, 1962, 1963, 1968, 1971, 1972, 1973, 1975, 1977, 1995 by The Lockman Foundation. Used by permission. (www.Lockman.org)

Verses marked NLT are taken from the Holy Bible, New Living Translation, copyright © 1996, 2004, 2015 by Tyndale House Foundation. Used by permission of Tyndale House Publishers, Inc., Carol Stream, Illinois 60188. All rights reserved.

Italicized text in Scripture quotations indicate authors' emphasis.

Cover design by Kyler Dougherty

Cover photo © ZU_09 / gettyimages

For bulk, special sales, or ministry purchases, please call 1-800-547-8979.
Email: Customerservice@hhpbooks.com

A Quick Reference Guide to the End Times
Copyright © 2020 by Text © Jeff Kinley and Todd Hampson. Artwork © Todd Hampson
Published by Harvest House Publishers
Eugene, Oregon 97408
www.harvesthousepublishers.com

ISBN 978-0-7369-8369-3 (pbk)
ISBN 978-0-7369-8370-9 (eBook)

Library of Congress Cataloging-in-Publication Data is on file at the Library of Congress, Washington, DC

All rights reserved. No part of this publication may be reproduced, stored in a retrieval system, or transmitted in any form or by any means—electronic, mechanical, digital, photocopy, recording, or any other—except for brief quotations in printed reviews, without the prior permission of the publisher.

Printed in the United States of America

20 21 22 23 24 25 26 27 28 / BP-CD / 10 9 8 7 6 5 4 3 2 1

CONTENTS

Exploring What the Bible Says About the End Times 5

1. What Is Bible Prophecy, and Why Is It Such a Big Deal? 7
2. In What Basic Order Will the End Times Unfold? 13
3. How Do We Know Jesus Is Literally Returning to Earth?... 19
4. What Is the Rapture, and Who Will Be Taken? 25
5. What Are the Signs of Christ's Return, and How Close Are We? 29
6. Has the Church Replaced Israel in God's Plans for the Future? 35
7. Is the Kingdom of God Already Here? 39
8. What Are the Different Views of the End Times, and Why Does It Matter? 45
9. How Can Bible Prophecy Help Convince Skeptics and Unbelievers? 51
10. How Should Christians Live if Jesus Might Return Any Day Now? 57

Endnotes 61

EXPLORING WHAT THE BIBLE SAYS ABOUT THE END TIMES

Welcome to *A Quick Reference Guide to Bible Prophecy*! This book will jump-start your study of Bible prophecy, providing answers to some of the key questions many people ask about the last days. We have designed this resource to serve as a quick yet comprehensive overview of the high points of Bible prophecy and how they relate to your life *right now*. Whether you're a pastor, small group leader, Sunday school teacher, involved in discipleship at the local church level, or you simply want to have a better understanding of God's plans for the future, this book is for you.

You are probably already aware that there are many books on Bible prophecy available. Trying to find one that covers the subject matter from a solidly biblical stance can be an overwhelming task. That's our commitment as The Prophecy Pros™—we want to let God's Word speak for itself on all matters relating to the end times so that we can be a trusted voice. We don't take that privilege lightly. We pray that as you use this resource, the Lord will deepen your love for His Word, give you clarity and confidence concerning the times in which we live, and fill you with hope regarding the incredible future God has for you, His child.

The Prophecy Pros™ came about because God moves in interesting ways and honors small steps of obedience. The two of us met through our book publishing endeavors and quickly realized we have a like-mindedness regarding Bible prophecy. That kindred spirit led to our desire to partner together in some strategic type of ministry—and just like that, The Prophecy Pros™ concept was born!

We share a burden to reach the next generation with the amazing message of Bible prophecy. In a world filled with more and more confusion, we are committed to equipping people with the resources to grow deeper in their understanding and application of God's truth. One of the ways we're doing this is through a single-day event called The Daniel Project: Thriving in the Lion's Den of Postmodern Culture.

In partnership with the incredible team at Harvest House Publishers, this book, along with the Prophecy Pros Podcast, is the result of our collective vision to produce vital new resources *for you* at a critical time when the world is looking for answers—answers that only God's prophetic Word can provide.

We trust you'll dig in and grow deep! As Zechariah 4:10 says, "Do not despise these small beginnings, for the LORD rejoices to see the work begin" (NLT).

May God enlighten your understanding and make you a discerner of the times as you continue seeking Him!

Jeff Kinley and Todd Hampson

Chapter 1

WHAT IS BIBLE PROPHECY, AND WHY IS IT SUCH A BIG DEAL?

When it comes to Bible prophecy, there is no shortage of speculation and sensationalism. You'll find everything from doomsday preachers predicting the end of the world to quirky "prophecy nerds" propagating conspiracy theories about the Antichrist and clandestine secret societies. Often there appears to be more confusion than clarity. But that's not the way God intended it.

Though there are some Bible prophecies that require deeper study to understand, most prophecies are relatively easy to grasp because God's Word is clear on much of what is said.

Defining Bible Prophecy

Very simply, Bible prophecy is God's plan revealed ahead of time. Like movie trailers, various prophecies offer sneak previews of things to come. But unlike a fictional movie, prophecy tells us what's *actually* going to happen. That's why some refer to it as history written in advance.

In the Old Testament, prophets were given truth about the future Messiah—His birth, ministry, death, and resurrection. In the New Testament, prophecies were proclaimed by John the Baptist, Jesus, Paul, Peter, and John, who addressed, from their perspective, events in both the near and distant future.

When we come to the last book in the Bible, we encounter an entire catalog of prophecies that have yet to be fulfilled. In Revelation 1:19, John was told to write down the things that "*will* take place" (in the future). It's important to note that only God can accurately foretell the future—not psychics, soothsayers, or even Satan himself.

The prophet Daniel declared, "There is a God in heaven who reveals mysteries, and He has made known to King Nebuchadnezzar what will take place *in the latter days*" (Daniel 2:28).

And God doesn't merely know what's going to take place. He actually causes these things to occur.[1] In Scripture, God revealed His future plans to His prophets in nearly every book of the Bible. He did this through dreams, visions, appearances, and direct revelation. Today, we have the completed revelation of God in Scripture, which includes about one thousand prophecies that relate to Jesus and the end times. Of these, around 500 are yet unfulfilled. Clearly, our God is a God of prophecy!

PROPHECY STATISTICS

- 28% OF THE BIBLE CONTAINS PROPHECY
- 1 OUT OF 30 VERSES CONTAINS PROPHECY
- 8000 TOTAL VERSES CONTAIN PROPHECY
- 23 OF 27 NEW TESTAMENT BOOKS MENTION THE RETURN OF CHRIST

Why We Should Care About Bible Prophecy

Still, we may wonder, "Why is prophecy such a big deal?" When reading, studying, or talking about the Bible, we typically spend a lot of time looking back to what God did in the past. But God also wants us to look forward to see what He is going to do in the future and to understand how that affects our lives today.

Here are seven compelling reasons Bible prophecy is so important:

1. Prophecy is *in the Bible*, and we know every verse is profitable for all believers (2 Timothy 3:16-17). This may sound a bit obvious, but if God chose to include something in Scripture, then it plays a strategic role in revealing God and His plans for history, humanity, and for His children.

2. Prophecy makes up about 28 percent of the entire Bible. Remove prophecy from God's Word, and you have gutted a significant portion of Scripture's supernatural character. Consider the following:

- One out of every 30 verses in the New Testament contains prophecy.
- There are 8,000 total verses that are prophetic in nature.
- Twenty-three out of 27 New Testament books mention the second coming of Jesus.
- For each verse that mentions the first coming of Jesus, there are *eight* verses that mention the second coming.
- The first prophecy about Christ appears in Genesis 3:15.
- There are 333 prophecies concerning Christ. Of those, 109 were fulfilled at his first coming. That leaves 224 prophecies yet to be fulfilled.

PROPHECIES ABOUT JESUS
333 TOTAL PROPHECIES
109 FULFILLED AT THE FIRST COMING
224 YET TO BE FULFILLED

3. According to Jesus, every word and letter of Scripture will eventually come to pass (Matthew 5:17-18). Every Old Testament prophecy about the Messiah was fulfilled literally and exactly as Scripture predicted. Given this perfect track record, it stands to reason that every future prophecy will also be fulfilled literally and exactly as the Bible foretells. The Bible is batting a thousand—it has never once missed on any point of a prophecy. Every single one so far has been fulfilled down to the most minute detail.[2] And the same will be true for the 500 prophecies with future fulfillments.

4. The last book of the Bible is 95 percent prophecy. Authors are very careful about how they end their books, considering the best ways to leave a lasting impact on the reader. God concluded His written revelation to man the same way. He could've ended His book any way He wanted, and yet He chose to do so by giving us a heads up on future history. Last words are lasting words. God

must want us to know about the future because His final word to us is all about that!

5. Another reason prophecy is such a big deal is because God doesn't want His children to be uninformed about the end times (1 Thessalonians 4:13; 2 Thessalonians 3:1-3, 5). But why? Because ignorance (or lack of information) leads to weakness. Ignorance about the future can give rise to fear, anxiety, and uncertainty. It also makes us vulnerable to misleading information, false teachers, errant beliefs, sensationalism, speculation, conspiracy theories, and baseless predictions. Thankfully, our fears about the future can be conquered by reading God's prophetic Word and trusting Him to accomplish it.

6. Prophecy is a big deal because of the times in which we live. At no time since Jesus walked the earth is end-times prophecy more likely to be fulfilled than it is right now. We will address this more in chapter 5, but the signs of the times—as described in Scripture—give every indication that we are living in the last days. And since Revelation's realities could be just around the corner, the relevance of Bible prophecy has never been more real to Christians.

7. Finally, prophecy really is a big deal because of what it does for you and me. Bible prophecy gives us:

- *Clarity* (2 Thessalonians 2:1-3, 5). Thanks to the Internet, virtually every person has unlimited access to thousands of views and opinions regarding the times in which we live and the future of humanity and planet earth. Scripture cuts through that fog, enlightening us to clear and specific truths about what lies ahead. This clarity frees us from confusion.

- *Confidence* (2 Thessalonians 2:1-3). Once you can clearly see what's ahead, you can proceed forward with confidence and assurance. You don't have to be timid about your beliefs concerning the rapture, the tribulation, the Antichrist, or Jesus' second coming. That's because prophetic Scripture gives insight and wisdom, enabling you to be strong in your beliefs.

- *Faith* (Revelation 4). The *strength* of our faith is directly proportionate to what we know about the *object* of our faith. If we know that God is on His throne guiding history toward its appointed end, then we can rest in knowing that not only does He hold the future, but us as well (Revelation 4). Studying prophecy *never* breeds fear. It only builds faith.
- *Hope* (Titus 2:13-15; 1 Thessalonians 4:13). In the Bible, hope is not a wish, but rather a confident expectation. Jesus' return for His bride is called the "blessed hope" (Titus 2:13). All throughout the New Testament there are dozens of verses that speak of the bride's expectation for that return.[3] And we know that hope will not be disappointed (Romans 5:4-5).
- *Love* for Jesus (Revelation 19:10). That's right—when you study Bible prophecy, it leads you straight to Jesus. That's because the ultimate point of prophecy is the Lord Jesus Christ. Bible prophecy reveals the character and heart of the God you worship. So, the more you study prophecy, the more you will be drawn into a closer and more intimate relationship with your Savior!

As you can see, God's prophetic plan for the future is a plan that greatly affects you as well. This is why Bible prophecy isn't on the "optional menu" for Christians, but rather is an essential part of our spiritual nourishment.

Chapter 2

IN WHAT BASIC ORDER WILL THE END TIMES UNFOLD?

There is no single passage in the Bible that lays out the exact order of all the key end-time events. However, there are several key passages of Scripture that allow us to piece together a very clear order of the major end-time events. If we begin with the premise that the Bible is God's (accurately given and faithfully preserved) Word, and that we can read and understand the plain sense of the text, then a clear order of key end-time events can be determined. Every single prophecy that has come to pass has been fulfilled literally, so we can deduce that all future prophecies will also be fulfilled literally.

With those concepts in mind, here is the basic order of key end-time events. We have also noted any significant alternate views in the descriptions that follow.

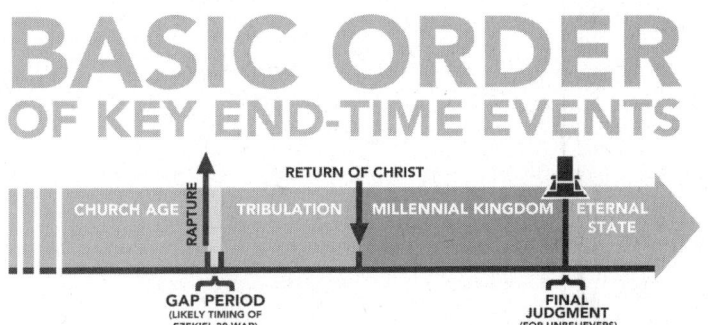

The Rapture

The rapture is a sign-less, imminent (could happen at any moment) future event. That's when all believers will be taken instantly to meet Jesus in the air, then go with Him to heaven (John 14:3; 1 Corinthians 15:52; 1 Thessalonians 4:15-18). The rapture and the resurrection are parts of the same event. There are no preconditions for this sudden, global, supernatural event. It is the next event on the prophetic calendar, and it will be the catalyst that sets all other future events in motion.

Gap Period

We learn in 2 Thessalonians 2:7-8 that the restrainer (the Holy Spirit, who indwells all church-age believers) must first be taken out of the way (via the rapture) before the man of sin (the Antichrist) can be revealed. Daniel chapter 9 informs us that the tribulation period begins when an agreement between Israel and "many" is finalized by the Antichrist (Daniel 9:27). Logic demands a gap period between the rapture and the beginning of the tribulation. This period could be minutes, hours, months, or possibly longer, though we tend to believe it will be relatively short—perhaps just a few weeks or months.

Ezekiel 38 War

Prophecy experts agree that this war is an end-time attack on Israel, but they vary on when they think it fits into the overall order of events. We believe this will be a post-rapture power grab led by Russia in partnership with Iran and Turkey, with support from Libya, Ethiopia, and Sudan. At the time of this writing (and for the first time in history), all of those nations are in partnership, aligned just as foretold in Scripture. Russia, Iran, and Turkey all have military assets in Syria.

This incredibly detailed prophecy (found in Ezekiel 38–39) about a yet-future attack on Israel is prophesied to occur after the nation has been a wasteland for a long period of time, with the people brought back from other nations and dwelling securely in the land (38:8). History records that during the Diaspora (the dispersion of the Jewish people around the world beginning in AD 70) and until Israel became a nation again in 1948, most of the area was a wasteland.

Today the land is flourishing, millions of Jewish people are back, and Israel is (as long prophesied) once again a nation. Israel is currently ranked the eighth most powerful nation in the world.[1] Though the Jewish people are surrounded by enemies, they have soundly defeated them in every conflict in modern times and, because of their military strength, currently live in safety within their national boundaries.

This future Ezekiel 38 attack will come from Israel's northern border, and the purpose of the invaders will be to steal something of value. Just within the last decade, Israel has discovered massive amounts of oil and natural gas reserves. For the first time in history, Israel is energy independent and has more than it could possibly need. So much so that the nation has planned and is building an undersea pipeline to sell energy to Europe, Russia's current largest customer.

Some prophecy experts believe a Psalm 83 war (an attack from Israel's border neighbors) must take place first, but this prophecy seems to have already been fulfilled through Israel's many defensive wars, including the War of Independence and the Six-Day War. Israel currently has peace agreements and emerging working relationships with her border neighbors (the Psalm 83 attackers)—a key detail that also lines up with Ezekiel 38 (specifically Saudi Arabia, known in the biblical text as Sheba and Dedan).

The Beginning of the Tribulation Period

In the chaotic aftermath of the rapture, when millions of Christians suddenly disappear, a world leader will emerge with the personality, charisma, political backing, and vision to restore world order. After the Ezekiel 38 war, the stage will also be set for this end-time ruler to rise to power (most likely from Europe—see Daniel 9:26) to broker a deal between Israel and "many" (Daniel 9:27). This deal will include permission for the Jewish people to rebuild the Jewish temple on the Temple Mount in Jerusalem.

The Midpoint of the Tribulation Period

Daniel chapter 9 informs us that the Antichrist will break his covenant with Israel at the exact midpoint of the seven-year period. He will defile the temple and turn on the Jewish people. This is also when the infamous mark of the beast will be implemented. The first half of the tribulation will be terrible, but the second half will be much worse for both the world's rebellious inhabitants and, unfortunately, most of the Jewish people alive at that time (Jeremiah 30:7; Daniel 12:1; Matthew 24:21). One bright spot during this period is that God will protect a number of the Jewish people, who will all turn to Christ as Savior at the end of the tribulation period (Daniel 12:1-2; Matthew 23:39; Romans 11:26; Revelation 12:14-17; Revelation 14:1-5).

The Return of Christ

The return of Christ is distinct from the rapture. At the rapture, church-age believers will be resurrected and transformed into their glorified spiritual bodies to meet Jesus in the air or clouds, then return with Him to heaven (John 14:3; 1 Corinthians 15:52; 1 Thessalonians 4:15-18). At the end of the tribulation period, Jesus will physically return to earth's surface with the armies of heaven (angels and church-age believers) following behind Him (Revelation 19:11-21). He will touch down on the Mount of Olives (Zechariah 14:4)—the same place from where He left (Acts 1:9-12), and the same place where He taught His disciples what would happen in the last days (Matthew 24; Mark 13; Luke 21).

KEY DIFFERENCES
BETWEEN THE RAPTURE AND THE RETURN

JESUS COMES IN THE AIR 1 Thess. 4:17	**JESUS COMES TO THE GROUND** Zech. 14:4; Acts 1:11
JESUS COMES FOR HIS OWN John 14:3; 1 Thess. 4:17	**JESUS COMES WITH HIS OWN** 1 Thess. 3:13; Rev. 19:14
DELIVERED FROM WRATH 1 Thess. 1:10	**BRINGS WRATH** Rev. 6:12-17; 19:15-21
PURPOSE—DELIVERANCE 1 Thess. 4:17-19; 5:9	**PURPOSE—JUDGMENT** Rev. 19:15-21
ONLY GOD KNOWS WHEN Matt. 24:36; 1 Cor. 15:50-54	**EXACTLY 7 YEARS AFTER TREATY** Daniel 9:27; Rev. 11:2-3; 12:6, 14; 13:5

The Millennial Kingdom

The Old Testament prophets (particularly Isaiah) foretold of a golden era when a descendant of David would rule the entire world from Jerusalem. We learn in Revelation 20:1-6 that this will be a 1,000-year period immediately following the tribulation (with a short time span allotted to transition to the kingdom age). While church-age believers will have been resurrected at the rapture (just prior to the tribulation), it appears that Old Testament era believers will be resurrected just before the millennial kingdom (Daniel 12:1-2; Isaiah 26:19; Revelation 20:4-6). The millennial kingdom will end with one final battle when Satan is released from prison. He will be quickly defeated and thrown permanently into the Lake of Fire (Revelation 20:7-10).

The Great White Throne Judgment

After the millennial kingdom, all nonbelievers throughout history will stand before God to be judged and, sadly, cast into the Lake of Fire. Believers will not stand before God at this judgment because their sins have been covered by the atonement of Jesus (Revelation 20:11-15).

The New Heaven and New Earth

Following the final judgment, all of creation will be completely renovated or recreated. Every bit of evil, sin, and decay will be removed from creation and new features will be added—one of which is the New Jerusalem. This is the heavenly city referred to in the book of Hebrews (11:10, 16), and most likely where each believer's custom-crafted living spaces are currently being constructed (John 14:3). The center of activity and God's presence will be in the New Jerusalem, but presumably we will be able to spend eternity traveling the vast areas of heaven.

As believers, we have an incredible multifaceted future to look forward to. This should motivate us to live faithfully for the Lord now in the face of struggle and temptation, and we should leverage every opportunity to point others to the Savior. These are things that we can do only during the present church age, and our labors will have ripple effects into eternity.

Chapter 3

HOW DO WE KNOW JESUS IS LITERALLY RETURNING TO EARTH?

Several years ago, I saw a bumper sticker that read, "Jesus Is Coming Back. Look Busy." Another one stated, "Jesus is coming back...and boy is He ticked off!"

Those stickers portray a Christ who is like an absent boss or a strict and overbearing parent, neither of which are accurate. It's true that He is returning, and He will indeed bring wrath when He comes. But beyond judgment, He is also coming to reign in righteousness (Revelation 19:11-21; 20:1-6; 22:12.)

Can We Be Certain About Jesus' Return?

The message of Christ's return has been on the lips of Jesus' bride for some 2,000 years. Today, a more updated sticker might read, "Jesus is coming back *soon*!"

But is He? And if so, how can we sure? How can we know His return is going to be an actual, *physical* appearance? Keep in mind we're talking about the second coming here, portrayed in Revelation 19, and not the rapture event, which we will discuss in the next chapter. These are two separate appearances.

To begin, consider that there are only three possibilities about how Jesus' second coming will occur:

1. He will return to planet earth.
2. He will not return at all.
3. He has already returned...kind of.

Of course, if Jesus is not coming back at all, then the discussion is effectively over. There is no way to verify this possibility because no one can definitively prove He's *not* coming back at some point. Granted, if His return is nothing more than a religious myth, then everything else the Bible claims about Jesus is also automatically questionable and suspect. For if we can't trust the scriptures that speak about the Lord's return, then how can we trust other passages when they speak of other important matters, such as morality, salvation, heaven, hell, and eternal life?

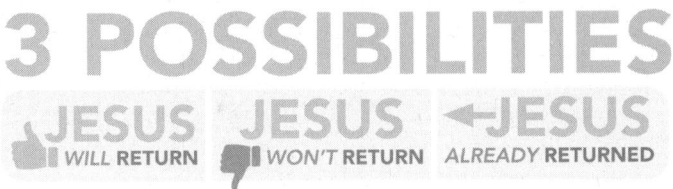

How Will Jesus Return?

However, if it's true that Christ *will* make another trip back to earth, then we are still faced with two potential options: (1) His return will be spiritual, not physical; or (2) He will indeed show up in a physical, glorified body.

The View Jesus' Return Is Spiritual

Let's first explore the view that sees Jesus' second coming as spiritual and not physical. Typically those who hold this belief fall under an interpretive view known as *preterism*. Preterism interprets the events described in Revelation chapters 6 to 19 as having already been fulfilled in AD 70 (or shortly after) when Jerusalem was destroyed by the Roman general Titus.[1]

Within this approach to Revelation are three subviews of preterism: mild, moderate, and extreme. Though all three see Revelation as being historically fulfilled in the first century, most preterists still believe in a future coming of Christ. However, extreme preterists believe He already returned in AD 70 and that it was a *spiritual* return, not a physical one.

It's obvious to all of us that Jesus did not arrive physically at Armageddon in the first century and slaughter the world's armies as described in Revelation 19:11-21. Therefore, for extreme preterists, His "return" must, of necessity, have been spiritual and symbolic in nature. In fact, preterists are forced to symbolize the majority of the prophecies and events in Revelation because there are no historical records or incidents that support the claim that the judgments described in Revelation 6 to 19 have ever occurred in Jerusalem, Israel, or anywhere in the world during the first century (or anywhere else since that time).[2]

If half the world's population had perished amid world wars and cataclysmic global judgments back then, you would expect that at least one person, scribe, or historian would have written this down (or even passed down the story orally). But there's nothing. Nada. Thus, preterists must spiritualize or symbolize virtually all the prophecies and events in Revelation in order for them to make sense according to their views.

The View Jesus' Return Is Literal

This leaves us with the second option (or interpretation): that the judgments described in Revelation 6 to 19 and Jesus' second coming are *literal*. And still yet future. Let's consider now the support for this perspective:

1. Jesus' birth and existence were literal. Virtually no historian or theologian today denies the historicity of Jesus Christ. The fact of his birth, life, and death are attested to by religious as well as secular historians, including the Jewish historian Josephus (b. AD 37), the Roman historian Tacitus (AD 56–120), Pliny the younger (b. AD 61), and scores of others.[3] To allege that Jesus never existed is to make a baseless and ignorant claim.

2. Jesus' resurrection was literal, involving a physical body. When Christ rose from the dead, He made it very clear to His followers that He possessed a physical body, though in a glorified, supernatural state (1 Corinthians 15:44). The Lord said in Luke

24:39, "Touch me and see; for a spirit does not have flesh and bones as you see that I have."

At the tomb, Mary clung to Jesus' physical body (John 20:17). Later that Sunday evening, He appeared to the disciples, showing them His hands and His side (John 20:20). Eight days later, Thomas was invited to touch his hands and side wounds (John 20:27-28). His resurrection was physical, bodily, and tangible.

3. Jesus promised to physically and literally return at the end of the age (Matthew 16:27; 24:30, 36, 42-44; Luke 21:34-36; Revelation 19:11-16). There are more than 200 references to this event in the New Testament, and not one of them hints at anything other than a physical return. Jesus Himself spoke of His return some 20 times.

4. The two angels at Jesus' ascension promised He would return physically to the same spot from which He ascended, announcing, "This Jesus...will come *in just the same way as you have watched Him go into heaven*" (Acts 1:11). At His physical ascension, we were promised a physical return.

5. Paul prophesied Jesus would be "*revealed* from heaven with His mighty angels in flaming fire" (2 Thessalonians 1:7).[4] Paul's words clearly communicate actual, not symbolic, language.

6. Scripture says Jesus' return will be *visible*, and that every eye will see Him when He comes on the clouds of heaven (Matthew 24:27-30; 26:64; Revelation 1:7).

7. The Bible references specific, geographical locations associated with His coming—places like Armageddon (Revelation 16:16), the Mount of Olives (Zechariah 14:3-4; Acts 1:9-11), and Jerusalem (Zechariah 12:1-3; 14:2; Revelation 16:17-21). These are real places that will welcome a real king on a real white horse (Revelation 19:11).

8. Literal (not symbolic or figurative) global armies will assemble to do battle at Armageddon against this returning Christ (Revelation 19:19-21).

9. A literal second coming of Jesus is what will usher in a literal 1,000-year millennial kingdom (Revelation 19–20).

10. Understanding Jesus' return is based on a literal approach to interpreting all of Scripture, including Revelation. The early church adopted this interpretive approach and expected any day to see the same Jesus who had left them for heaven years earlier.[5]

100% OF THE 1ST COMING PROPHECIES WERE FULFILLED LITERALLY

100% OF THE 2ND COMING PROPHECIES WILL BE FULFILLED LITERALLY

The second coming of Jesus Christ is the climax of Revelation's prophetic narrative. It marks the crescendo of human history, a red-letter date on God's calendar. If we can't trust it to be real, then how can we trust anything else in Revelation to be true? Therefore, by all indications, the Bible prophesies a literal, future, physical return of our Lord Jesus Christ.

Chapter 4

WHAT IS THE RAPTURE, AND WHO WILL BE TAKEN?

The rapture is a supernatural future event when the entire church (all true believers all over the world) will suddenly be "caught up" to be with the Lord Jesus Christ. The New Testament Greek word used to speak of the rapture is *harpazó*, which means "to seize, catch up, snatch away."[1] The concept is connected to a powerful and open display of force, or taking a prize away from an enemy—and doing so quickly and without warning. This event will remove the church from earth immediately prior to a time of God's judgment known as the tribulation period (see Revelation 3:10 on pages 26-27). Every single church-age believer (living and dead), and every person unable to discern right from wrong (the unborn, young children, etc.) will be taken in the rapture.

This mind-blowing future event is one that all Christians should long for and look forward to. In a split second, all church-age believers will be freed from sin and enter the presence of the Lord. The rapture is clearly taught in Scripture and is designed to give all believers great hope and joy. We are to live with this expectation and told to "encourage one another with these words" (see 1 Thessalonians 4:18 on page 26).

The word *rapture* itself is not found in Scripture, but is a transliteration of the Latin word *rapturo*, which translates the Greek term *harpazó*. Referring to this future event as the rapture has become more familiar to Christians than calling it "the *harpazó*," which means "the snatching away," or "the catching away."

At the moment of the rapture, Christians who have already died will be resurrected and transformed into their glorified eternal bodies.

Immediately following this, all believers who are still alive on earth with be instantly transformed into their eternal bodies and caught up along with the resurrected believers. Together, both groups of church-age believers will instantly join Jesus in the clouds—in the heart of enemy territory—and will then return with Him to heaven.

The Scripture Passages

Here are the primary texts that describe the rapture:

1 Thessalonians 4:16-18

> The Lord himself will come down from heaven, with a loud command, with the voice of the archangel and with the trumpet call of God, and the dead in Christ will rise first. After that, we who are still alive and are left will be caught up together with them in the clouds to meet the Lord in the air. And so we will be with the Lord forever. Therefore encourage one another with these words.

1 Corinthians 15:51-53

> Listen, I tell you a mystery: We will not all sleep, but we will all be changed—in a flash, in the twinkling of an eye, at the last trumpet. For the trumpet will sound, the dead will be raised imperishable, and we will be changed. For the perishable must clothe itself with the imperishable, and the mortal with immortality.

John 14:3

> If I go and prepare a place for you, I will come back and take you to be with me that you also may be where I am.

Revelation 3:10

> Since you have kept my command to endure patiently, I will also keep you from the hour of trial that is going

to come on the whole world to test the inhabitants of the earth.

Harpazó is used 13 times in the New Testament, and the context is always a sudden and forceful snatching up, catching away, or taking by force (see Matthew 11:12; 13:19; John 6:15; 10:12; 10:28; 10:29; Acts 8:39; 23:10; 2 Corinthians 12:2; 12:4; 1 Thessalonians 4:17; Jude 23; Revelation 12:5).

The Primary Views

There are different views regarding the timing of the rapture (in relation to the future seven-year period of God's judgment on earth known as the tribulation). The most common views (according to recent studies[2]) among Christians are the pre-tribulation rapture view and the post-tribulation rapture view (with the pre-tribulation view having about double the number of adherents as the post-tribulation view).

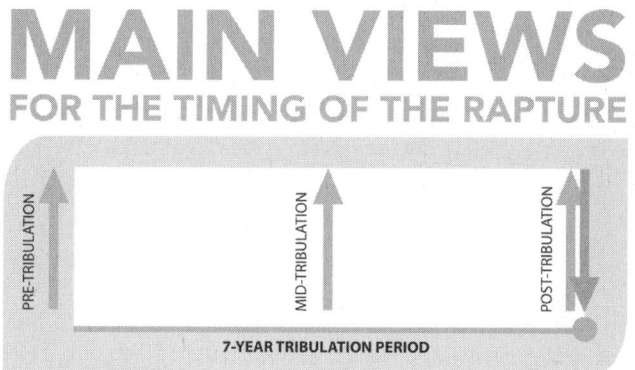

There are several reasons to have confidence in the pre-tribulation view: First, it is the only view that allows the rapture to be imminent (meaning it could happen at any moment throughout the church age). This is important because there are no prophecies in Scripture that need to be fulfilled before the rapture happens. It is the next event on God's prophetic calendar.

Second, it is the only view that can be used to "encourage one another," as seen in 1 Thessalonians 4:18. In other words, the rapture is encouraging only if we escape the wrath to come. Scripture clearly teaches that we are not appointed to wrath (Romans 5:9; 1 Thessalonians 1:10; Revelation 3:10)—and it also clearly teaches that the entire tribulation period (from the first seal judgment onward) is a time of God's wrath (Revelation 6:1, 16-17; 19:11-21).

Another reason is that we are told that we will be kept *from* the world's hour of trial (Revelation 3:10). The pattern of God's judgment, as revealed in the Old Testament, always shows God removing the righteous prior to the outpouring of His judgment (for example, Noah and Lot).

Finally, a pretribulation rapture mirrors the ancient Jewish wedding traditions hinted at by Jesus in John 14:3, whereby the groom would become engaged to a bride, go back to his father's house to prepare a home for her, then return suddenly to take her away to her new home.

The Purposes

By the way, in the Old Testament, trumpets were used to call the Israelites to assembly—to gather them together. Paul uses this symbology to convey that this—the last trumpet—is the final call to order of the church age. This is not to be confused with the trumpet judgments in Revelation, which John mentioned about 50 years after Paul's epistles were written.

The rapture of the church will serve as the exclamation point of the church age. It will fulfill God's promises and will separate all believers from sin and judgment. It was one of the mysteries of the church age revealed to Paul the apostle and is designed to produce hope, joy, perseverance, and excited anticipation in all of us who are believers as we await the Bridegroom to whisk away the church, His bride.

Chapter 5

WHAT ARE THE SIGNS OF CHRIST'S RETURN, AND HOW CLOSE ARE WE?

When you hear people refer to end-time signs, they are generally talking about one of two things. First, they may be referring to specific signs we were told to look for that signal the nearness of Christ's return. Second, they may be talking about specific world conditions forming in our day that mirror the conditions described in Bible prophecy. These conditions are logically necessary for key events to occur during the future seven-year tribulation period (also known as the Day of the Lord).

One key section of Scripture detailing what to look for during the end times is the Olivet Discourse (Matthew 24–25; Mark 13; Luke 21). This extended and detailed teaching by Jesus was delivered in response to specific questions the disciples asked about the time of the end. Aside from the book of Revelation, the Olivet Discourse is the longest passage about end-time prophecies in the New Testament. It is also the second-longest continuous teaching by Jesus recorded in Scripture (the longest being the Sermon on the Mount). The key point to note here is that Jesus did not rebuke His disciples for asking about the signs that would indicate the end was drawing near. Rather, He provided a lengthy teaching containing many details.

While no one but God the Father knows the day or hour of Christ's future return (Matthew 24:36), we are told in Hebrews 10:25 that Christians will be able to see "the Day approaching." "The Day" refers to the Day of the Lord, or the tribulation period. This is a future seven-year period of God's judgment on earth. We are also told that the unbelieving world will be caught off guard when the Lord comes "like a thief" (1 Thessalonians 5:2), but Christians will not (verse 4).

We should also note that the rapture and the return are two different events. The rapture will occur prior to the beginning of the tribulation period, and the return of Christ to earth will occur at the end. There's an often-used analogy that helps as we watch for the signs of the Lord's return. When you see Christmas decorations going up but Thanksgiving has not arrived yet, then you know Thanksgiving must be coming very soon. Similarly, when we see signs that the tribulation period is around the corner, we know that the rapture of the church is even closer.

The Categories

The simplest way to provide an overview of the signs is to list and discuss them by category. The categories below mention the various signs and conditions we are to watch for as we await the Lord's return. They are indicators of the nearness of the Lord's return.

The Super Sign—Israel's Rebirth as a Nation

Many prophecy experts call Israel's rebirth "the super sign." They do this mainly for two reasons. First, all other end-time signs hinge on this one. No other sign of the end could occur until Israel became a nation again. Second, experts call Israel's rebirth the super sign because of the sheer magnitude of this sign coming to pass. It is statistically impossible to predict this sign with all its details and necessary preconditions and have it fulfilled in every detail as it has been in our modern era.

The reestablishment of the nation of Israel occurred on May 14,

1948. Every Old Testament prophet except Jonah predicted that Israel would become a nation again and that Jewish people from around the world would return to their ancient homeland.

Israel's rebirth is the main aspect of this super sign, but there are many other end-time signs associated with it. Several prophecies regarding events leading up to and after her rebirth in our modern era (beginning in the late 1800s) were predicted in Scripture.

Geopolitical Signs

In addition to rebirth of the nation of Israel, the Bible also predicts several other specific geopolitical conditions. For example, in Ezekiel 38 we learn of an end-time attack on Israel after her rebirth. This is one of the most detailed prophecies in the Bible, and it mentions an end-time alignment of nations involving Russia, Turkey, and Iran, who will work together to lead a military coalition against Israel.

Russia is said to be the leader/protector and the combined forces are prophesied to attack from the northern mountains of Israel (that is, from Syria, but Syria will not be a player in the attack) for the purpose of taking something valuable from Israel. This end-time attack (which God will quickly and supernaturally squash) will be protested by Saudi Arabia (38:13—Sheba and Dedan) along with "Tarshish and all her villages" (literally, "young lions/strong lions"). Many prophecy experts make a strong case that Tarshish is modern-day England (or possibly Spain), making her villages ("young lions") nations that grew out of the British Empire—including America. If this is the case, it appears from this prophecy that America will not be in a position to assist Israel militarily.

The stage for this scenario is fully set. The Arab Spring and the civil war in Syria (beginning in 2011) became the catalysts for Russia, Iran, and Turkey to fill the political and military void in Syria. These led to an official partnership between the three nations—along with the other secondary nations listed in the Ezekiel 38 prophecy, such as Libya and Sudan.

There are many other geopolitical end-time signs, including the political push for a global government (United Nations and other globalist organizations), the foundation for a revived Roman Empire (European Union), and the emergence of Far East nations as superpowers (such as China). All these developments relate to specific end-time prophecies and were predicted thousands of years ago.

Natural Signs

In the Olivet Discourse, Jesus listed various signs of nature that would increase in frequency and intensity (like birth pains) as we get closer to the time of the end. Pause for a moment and think about the number of unprecedented weather and seismic events that have taken place in the past 10 to 15 years. It seems that with each catastrophic event we hear terms such as *unprecedented, once-in-a-lifetime,* or *once-in-a-century* used to describe what happened.

Haiti. Japan. Indonesia. Chile. Pakistan. In recent memory, these are some of the places that have experienced major earthquakes that caught the world's attention due to the quakes' destructive power, the resulting tsunamis, the staggering loss of life, and horrific video footage. The 9.3 Indian Ocean earthquake and tsunami in 2004 killed 230,000-280,000 people. It was the third most powerful quake ever recorded and it had the longest duration ever noted.

Extreme weather and seismic activity are the natural result of a fallen world that groans in anticipation of redemption (Romans 8:22-23). And the Lord foreknew that as the earth continued to *wear out like a garment* (Isaiah 51:6), the birth pains of its growing instability would noticeably increase in the lead up to the appointed end.

Spiritual Signs

There are positive and negative spiritual signs to look for. On the positive side, according to Bible prophecy, we should expect to see more Jewish people accept Jesus as their Messiah (Matthew 23:39; Romans 11:26; Revelation 7:4) and the gospel going to all nations (Matthew 24:14).

On the negative side, we should expect to see apostasy (a falling away from truth) in the church at large (2 Timothy 3:1-5); the rise of false Christs, cults, and spiritual deception (Matthew 24:24); persecution of Jews and Christians (Matthew 24:9); scoffers (2 Peter 3:3-4); and the rise of the occult (Revelation 9:21).

These spiritual trends will reach their apex during the tribulation period, with both sides of the spectrum of spiritual conditions being on full display. Revelation informs us that occult practices and demonic activity will be prevalent around the world. At the same time, 144,000 Jewish evangelists will be boldly proclaiming the gospel throughout the world. Vast numbers of people will choose to follow Christ and will thoroughly commit themselves to Him—many to the point of martyrdom.

Cultural Signs

This single passage sums it up powerfully when it comes to cultural signs:

> Mark this: There will be terrible times in the last days. People will be lovers of themselves, lovers of money, boastful, proud, abusive, disobedient to their parents, ungrateful, unholy, without love, unforgiving, slanderous, without self-control, brutal, not lovers of the good, treacherous, rash, conceited, lovers of pleasure rather than lovers of God (2 Timothy 3:1-4).

Read that description and think of the current conditions in culture. This 2,000-year-old prophecy reads like a modern-day account of what people are like in today's world.

Technological Signs

Many predictions in Scripture point to advanced technology that is necessary for certain future events to occur. When the prophets of old delivered the messages and visions they received from the Lord, often they did not understand the details within the prophecies. From a technology standpoint, the fulfillment of many prophecies was not even possible at the time they were given.

Nuclear weaponry, satellite and Internet broadcasting, massive data centers, DNA manipulation, artificial intelligence, surveillance systems, transhumanism, and many other current and emerging technologies are described in Bible prophecy or are logically necessary for end-time events to occur. Today, every technology needed to fulfill end-time prophecies exists!

Convergence

Another oft-used analogy to describe the nearness of the end times is that of a play about to start. You look around the theatre and see that everyone is getting into their seats and the house is full. The curtain on the stage is still closed, but under the curtain you can see feet shuffling around on the stage. You hear lots of commotion and you can tell props are being set up. All you are waiting for are the lights to dim and the curtain to open—then it's showtime.

The fact that every single end-time sign category is in active play in our day should get our attention. Never before in history has there been such a convergence of events and conditions.

How Close?

All these sign categories—particularly that of convergence—means that we are likely very close to the Lord's return. As we mentioned above, Scripture is clear that no man knows the day or the hour (Matthew 24:36), but we can study the many signs and know that His return is drawing near (Matthew 24:33; Luke 21:28; Hebrews 10:25).

Chapter 6

HAS THE CHURCH REPLACED ISRAEL IN GOD'S PLANS FOR THE FUTURE?

The church has not replaced Israel, and the Jews are still God's chosen people. This is a very important aspect of end-time Bible prophecy. Some of God's promises to Israel were conditional, based on their obedience—with prophesied consequences if they disobeyed (Deuteronomy 28). They did disobey, and those consequences came to pass. In addition to the conditional promises, God also gave many specific and unconditional promises to (and prophecies about) Israel.

In Genesis 15:12-19, God made a one-way unconditional covenant with Abraham about several things, including the promise of the land of Israel to Abraham's descendants. All through history, Israel has never occupied the full breadth of the land specified by God (from the Nile River to the Euphrates River) in this ancient unconditional covenant.

There are also many specific prophecies (for example, in Psalms, Isaiah, Jeremiah, Ezekiel, Daniel, Hosea, Micah, Matthew, Luke, and Revelation) about a future golden age when the Messiah will rule the entire world from Jerusalem, the animal kingdom will have no carnivores, and the topography of Jerusalem will change completely.

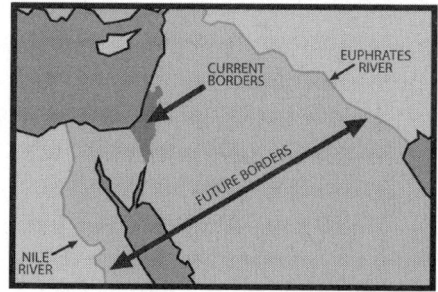

These kingdom prophecies obviously have not happened yet. They will be fulfilled in the future millennial kingdom after the seven-year tribulation period. These clear and specific prophetic details (which make up a sizeable portion of Scripture) would have to be allegorized, ignored, or intentionally explained away if God does not have future plans for Israel.

The Permanence of God's Promises

If there were any doubt about the permanence of God's program for the Jewish people, in Genesis 17:7 God said in crystal-clear terms, "I will establish my covenant as an everlasting covenant between me and you and your descendants after you for the generations to come, to be your God and the God of your descendants after you."

In response to those who say God has rejected His chosen people, Jeremiah 33:25-26 records God's clear declaration, where He essentially says, "I would no more reject my people than I would change my laws that govern night and day, earth and sky." In the New Testament, Paul echoes this fact in Romans 11:1-2, where he asks (and answers) the rhetorical question, "Did God reject his people? By no means! I am an Israelite myself, a descendant of Abraham, from the tribe of Benjamin. God did not reject his people, whom he foreknew."

Paul concludes this section of Romans (about the difference between God's program for Israel and the church) by pointing to a future day at the end of the church age when Israel will corporately turn to the true Messiah for salvation. In Romans 11:25-26, he says, "I do not want you to be ignorant of this mystery, brothers and sisters, so that you may not be conceited: Israel has experienced a hardening in part until the full number of the Gentiles has come in, and in this way all Israel will be saved." Paul was referring to the future moment Jesus prophesied about in Matthew 23:39: "I tell you, you will not see me again until you say, 'Blessed is he who comes in the name of the Lord.'"

Individually, all people must accept Christ as their Savior in order to be saved (Acts 4:12; Romans 3:23-31; 10:1, 4). Corporately, God has very distinct purposes for the church and for Israel. If God breaks His unconditional promises to Israel, how can we trust His unconditional promises to the church?

The Primary Views

There are primarily three approaches to understanding the relationship between the church and Israel. *Replacement theology* teaches that the church has replaced Israel and that all the promises given to Israel are now conferred onto the church. *Covenant Theology* teaches that the church is an expansion or offshoot of Israel. Neither of these views consistently interprets Bible prophecy in a literal manner.

The third approach, which I believe is the correct one, is that the Bible should be consistently interpreted literally from Genesis to Revelation. The conclusions from this approach clearly demonstrate that God has two distinct programs—one for Israel, and one for the church. The term used to describe this approach is *dispensationalism*. It squares with Scripture and teaches that individual salvation is by grace through faith, but also that God still has distinct purposes (and yet-unfulfilled future prophecies) for both groups. Israel and the church will merge beautifully in the future millennial kingdom and ultimately in the eternal state.

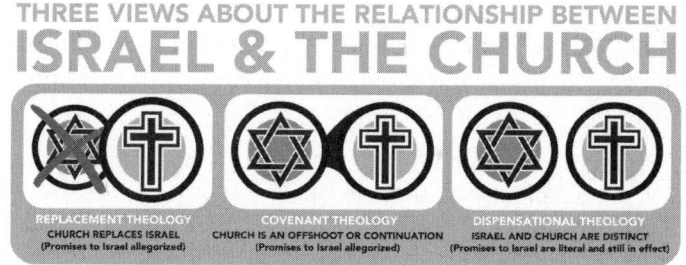

All 3 views believe in a personal decision to follow Christ for salvation.

Israel Is Key to End-Time Prophecies

When it comes to end-time prophecies, Israel and the Jewish people play a major role. As mentioned in chapter 5, prophecy experts refer to Israel's rebirth as the super sign of the end times for two reasons. First, because all other end-time events hinge on this one sign being in place. And second, because of the sheer magnitude and impossibility of this rebirth taking place by chance or historical coincidence.

Every Old Testament prophet except Jonah prophesied that Israel would be reborn. Consider these verses written 2,600 years ago:

> *Jeremiah 16:14-15*—"'However, the days are coming,' declares the Lord, 'when it will no longer be said, "As surely as the Lord lives, who brought the Israelites up out of Egypt," but it will be said, "As surely as the Lord lives, who brought the Israelites up out of the land of the north and out of all the countries where he had banished them." For I will restore them to the land I gave their ancestors.'"
>
> *Ezekiel 36:24*—"I will take you out of the nations; I will gather you from all the countries and bring you back into your own land."
>
> *Isaiah 11:11*—"In that day the Lord will reach out his hand a second time to reclaim the surviving remnant of his people."

The final book of the Bible, Revelation, highlights the end of the church age and how God's focus will shift back to Israel. In the 404 verses that appear in Revelation, there are more than 800 direct references to the Old Testament. We also find 2 Jewish witnesses, 144,000 Jewish evangelists, and a clear focus on Israel, Jerusalem, and an end-time Jewish temple.

During the tribulation period, the church will be with Jesus in heaven (Revelation 4:1, 4-5, 9-11) while God judges the evil world system and focuses on turning the hearts of the Jewish people to the true Messiah (Revelation 7:1-8; 11:3-12; 12:1-6; 14:1-4).

After the tribulation, the church and Israel will blend together in a beautiful way. In eternity, God will set up a city known as the New Jerusalem. It will feature 12 gates bearing the names of the 12 tribes of Israel (Revelation 21:12), and 12 foundations featuring the names of the 12 apostles (verse 14). Israel (all Jewish people who accepted Christ) and the church (all non-Jewish people who accepted Christ) will merge seamlessly and enjoy God's presence together for all eternity.

Chapter 7

IS THE KINGDOM OF GOD ALREADY HERE?

What comes to your mind when you hear the phrase *kingdom of God*? Chances are you've prayed the Lord's prayer at some point, reciting the words, "Your kingdom come. Your will be done, on earth as it is in heaven" (Matthew 6:10). But have you ever wondered what that kingdom actually is? And when, if ever, it's going to come? Or what it's going to be like? Do you picture God on His throne in heaven? Or do images of some future glory fill your mind? Perhaps you've been led to believe His kingdom is not some future reality, but rather here and now.

What Scripture Says About the Kingdom

The Old Testament

As far back as the Old Testament, God's kingdom was a prevalent theme. King David prayed,

> Yours, O Lord, is the greatness and the power and the glory and the victory and the majesty, indeed everything that is in the heavens and the earth; Yours is the dominion, O Lord, and You exalt Yourself as head over all. Both riches and honor come from You, and You rule

over all, and in Your hand is power and might; and it lies in Your hand to make great and to strengthen everyone (1 Chronicles 29:11-12).

King Nebuchadnezzar confessed, "His dominion is an everlasting dominion, and His kingdom endures from generation to generation" (Daniel 4:34). King Darius declared, "He is the living God and enduring forever, and His kingdom is one which will not be destroyed, and His dominion will be forever" (Daniel 6:26).

The psalmists agreed:

- "The LORD is King forever and ever" (10:16).
- "The LORD reigns…Your throne is established from of old" (93:1-2).
- "The LORD is a great God, and a great King above all gods" (95:3).
- "Say among the nations, 'The LORD reigns'" (96:10).
- "Our God is in the heavens; He does whatever He pleases" (115:3).

The prophet Isaiah wrote, "A child will be born to us, a son will be given to us; and the government will rest on His shoulders" (Isaiah 9:6).

The Old Testament portrays God as a mighty ruler over His kingdom. And when we get to the Gospels, we hear about more specific and immediate aspects of this kingdom.

The New Testament

John the Baptist and Jesus both heralded, "Repent, for the kingdom of heaven is at hand." (Matthew 3:2; 4:17). Jesus went on to say,

- "The kingdom of God is in your midst" (Luke 17:21).
- "My kingdom is not of this world" (John 18:36).
- "To you it has been granted to know the mysteries of the kingdom of heaven" (Matthew 13:11).

Scripture also says that believers will one day reign upon the earth with Christ (Revelation 3:21; 5:10; 20:4, 6; 22:5).

The Extent of God's Kingdom

So is God's kingdom here, there, or *everywhere*? The simple answer is yes, yes, and yes!

This can seem a bit complex. Further complicating matters is the fact that Satan also claims a kingdom of his own.

> [The devil] led Him up and showed Him all the kingdoms of the world in a moment of time. And the devil said to Him, "I will give you all this domain and its glory; for it has been handed over to me, and I give it to whomever I wish" (Luke 4:5-6).

What is interesting here is that Jesus did not challenge Satan's claim to the kingdoms of the world, but rather acknowledged it (John 12:31; 14:30; 16:11). John would later write, "The whole world lies in the power of the evil one" (1 John 5:19).

So, whose world is it—God's, or Satan's? If you're feeling a bit confused, don't despair. There is a way to better understand all this. Usually when the Bible speaks of God's kingdom, it's referring to His sovereignty or rule over all there is. From eternity past, God has always reigned supremely. He ruled in heaven before the creation of the universe. And when He made Adam, He designated him as coruler over the earth and the animal kingdom (Genesis 1:26-28). Unfortunately, Adam forfeited his privileged status when he and wife Eve sinned in the garden. As a result, instead of subduing the earth and ruling over the animals, man would serve the earth, toiling the ground for his food (Genesis 3:17-19).

God's rightful rule over His creation was again challenged during the sin-soaked days of Noah, and God responded again with judgment, this time sending a global flood that wiped out humanity (Genesis 6–9). Eventually He reestablished His kingdom program through a special relationship with the Jewish nation of Israel. This relationship was facilitated through various "promise agreements" (or covenants) He made with Abraham (Genesis 12:1-3; 15:1-21) and David (2 Samuel 7:14).

In time, God sent His Son to be their Messiah. Jesus came, presenting Himself to the Jewish nation as their righteous King. This is why both He and John the Baptist spoke of God's kingdom as being "near" and "in your midst" (Luke 17:31; John 18:36). However, instead of embracing God's Son as their prophesied King, Israel rejected Him and His offer of the kingdom (Matthew 12:24; 21:43-44). The apostle John records, "He came to His own, and those who were His own did not receive Him" (John 1:11).

As a result, the long-awaited fulfillment of God's promised kingdom would have to be postponed until a later time. In fact, the entire church age and future tribulation period will pass before future aspects of God's kingdom will be realized for Israel (Isaiah 60:1-22; Romans 11:26-27).

The Expression of God's Kingdom

Two very important expressions of this kingdom are

1. *Christ's 1,000-year millennial kingdom* (Psalm 2:6-9; Daniel 7:13-14; Zechariah 14:9; Revelation 20). In Revelation 20, six times in seven verses John repeats the phrase "a thousand years" (verses 2,3,4,5,6,7). He does this to make these points: this kingdom is literal, and it will literally run 1,000 years in length. The Latin translation of this phrase "a thousand years" is the word *millennium*. This earthly, physical reign of Christ will be characterized not only by His kingly sovereignty (Isaiah 11:4), but also by righteousness (Isaiah 11:3-5; 32:1) and holiness (Zechariah 14:20-21). We'll talk more about this millennial kingdom in chapter 9.

2. *The eternal kingdom* (Exodus 15:18; Hebrews 1:8). This refers to God's rule extending forever without interruption or challenge (1 Corinthians 15:23-28).

The seventh angel sounded; and there were loud voices in heaven, saying, "The kingdom of the world has become the kingdom of our Lord and of His Christ; and He will reign forever and ever." And the twenty-four elders, who sit on their thrones before God, fell on their faces and worshiped God, saying, "We give You thanks, O Lord God, the Almighty, who are and who were, because You have taken Your great power and have begun to reign" (Revelation 11:15-17).

In the new heavens and new earth, Jesus will reign as King forever and ever! (Psalms 9:7; 146:10; 2 Peter 3:13).

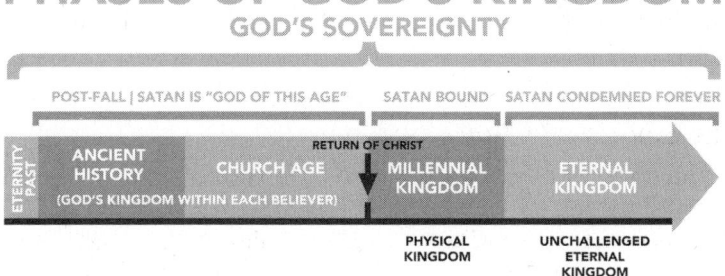

Taking Part in God's Kingdom

If that refers to the future establishment of God's kingdom, in what sense is His kingdom here and now? And how do we take part in it?

First, know that God has never stopped ruling over the universe. He always has and always will (Psalm 47:8; 93:1-5). Even though Satan is currently allowed to function as the "god of this world" (2 Corinthians 4:4), the Lord is still sovereign over the devil and all evil. And at Jesus' return, He will officially put an end to all satanic and demonic rule. At the start of the millennial kingdom, God will claim all of Satan's domain, taking back for all time what is rightfully

His as "KING OF KINGS, AND LORD OF LORDS" (Revelation 19:16). Satan's earthly kingdom will be no more.

Second, God also reigns as King in believers' hearts and in the church, over which he is the head (Colossians 1:18; 1 Peter 3:15).

While here on earth, Christians live under the rule (kingdom) of Christ, who has rescued us from the dominion (kingdom) of darkness (Colossians 1:13-14). While our allegiance used to be to Satan and self, we now submit to the one we've declared our Master and King (Matthew 23:8-10; Colossians 3:24). This reality inspires us to lead the kind of life that is worthy of this kingdom (1 Thessalonians 2:13). This is a kingdom characterized not by clever words or philosophies, but by the power of the Holy Spirit working in and through us right now (1 Corinthians 2:1-5; 4:20).

It then becomes our privilege to serve the Lord in His kingdom by helping others come to know Him through salvation by faith in Christ (Matthew 6:33; Acts 28:31; 2 Corinthians 5:20).

Whether in the past with Israel, the present through the church, or in the future through Christ's reign and reestablished Davidic throne, God's kingdom manifests itself in various forms and expressions. And in every way, God remains the unrivalled sovereign over the universe.

Chapter 8

WHAT ARE THE DIFFERENT VIEWS OF THE END TIMES, AND WHY DOES IT MATTER?

Have you ever wondered why there are so many views about the end times? Why there is such division and disagreement among Bible scholars and godly men? And given the fact such disagreement exists, does that mean one's view of the end times is unimportant, or perhaps even optional? Is it really necessary that we hold to a specific view of the rapture, Jesus' return, and the millennial kingdom? Or should we leave our options open and let God sort out the details?

Let's begin by stating the obvious: Because God has put so much information about these events in His Word, they must be important to Him…and therefore to us. And because all Scripture is profitable for us, the teachings about the last days and Christ's return are by no means minor or marginal topics.

Second, to say one's view of a certain doctrine is unimportant just because there is disagreement about it is to devalue not only the doctrine, but the very Word of God itself. There are many important teachings in the Bible about which there has been enormous debate and disagreement over the centuries, but this reality doesn't in any way diminish the importance of those doctrines.

At the same time, a person's view of the end times in no way reflects upon that person's salvation or relationship with Jesus Christ. God does not require someone to believe a specific view about the timing of the rapture to become a Christian. It also doesn't mean that some people are better Christians than others just because they hold to a certain view. Even so, because prophetic statements appear in the Bible, they definitely matter.

What are the various views? How do people arrive at these perspectives? And which views make the most sense biblically?

Your Approach to Interpreting the Bible Will Affect Your View

An important principle to remember is that your belief regarding the end times is determined by your approach to interpreting Scripture. Interpreting the Bible (hermeneutics) is a discipline that has serious implications. How you approach the interpretation of God's Word will determine your destination.

For example, when a plane is approaching a runway, it must line up properly with certain marker points or it could miss the runway altogether. The pilot must preset his coordinates, then make sure he stays on course the entire way. If he is off at the beginning of his journey, then he will likely miss the runway, the airport, and perhaps even the city he is aiming for. The same is true with interpreting the Bible and prophecy. How you begin will determine where you end up. If you begin with a flawed approach, you will certainly miss the "runway" (that is, the meaning of the passage).

Traditionally, there have been two general methods to studying the end times: the literal and the allegorical methods. The literal approach takes the biblical passage at face value, assuming it says what it means and means what it says. A good rule of Bible study is this: When the plain sense of Scripture makes common sense, seek no other sense lest you end up with *nonsense*!

The allegorical approach, on the other hand, sees Scripture's words as pointing to something else, usually some deeper spiritual or symbolic meaning. Often what happens is this meaning ends up being arbitrarily determined by the interpreter. Because the meaning is considered allegorical, different students may come up with different meanings.

The literal approach will lead you to specific views regarding Revelation and the end times, whereas the allegorical approach will lead you to a multitude of possible views. Later in this chapter, we'll observe how these methods work.

Four Main Views of the End Times and Revelation

The four most popular views of Revelation and the end times are as follows:

1. *The Preterist View*—Revelation already happened in the first century. Its prophecies have been fulfilled. Jesus returned in AD 70 and Satan has already been cast into the Lake of Fire.

2. *The Historicist View*—End-time prophecies have been fulfilled since the first century and throughout church history. This is the weakest and least popular view.

3. *The Symbolic View*—Daniel and Revelation are spiritualized to mean just about anything you want them to. In this view, none of the prophecies are fulfilled literally, but rather point to deeper spiritual meanings (for example, the Antichrist and false prophet are not real persons but signify the principle of evil, and Armageddon is not a real battle but pictures the spiritual battle of good [God] versus evil).

4. *The Futurist View*—The prophecies in Revelation have not been fulfilled yet. When they are, they will occur exactly as described in the book. This view does not discount symbols or figures of speech when they occur, but recognizes that John typically points out those figures of speech when he uses them—such as in Revelation 11:8 (the great city, Sodom, is Jerusalem); 5:8 (bowls of incense are prayers); 12:1-2 (the woman and child are Israel and Christ); 12:6, 14 ("a time and times and half a time" is 1,260 days); 17:1, 18 (great prostitute is Babylon); 17:12 (ten horns are ten kings); 17:9-12 (seven kings/heads are 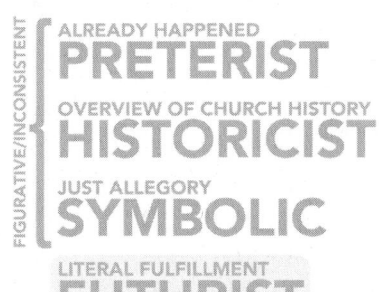 easily explained by looking at history from John's first-century perspective).

Of the four views described above, only the futurist takes a literal approach to interpreting Scripture. Because every one of the prophecies concerning Jesus' first coming were fulfilled literally and exactly as portrayed in Scripture, it makes sense to anticipate that future prophecies will be fulfilled literally as well. None of the first-coming prophecies were fulfilled figuratively or symbolically.

Varying Views of the Rapture and Millennium

Three Views of the Rapture

Beliefs concerning the blessed hope (Titus 2:13) all have to do with *timing*. In other words, all these views believe in the rapture but differ as to *when* Jesus will come and rescue His bride.

- The pre-tribulation view says that Christ will return *prior* to the time of tribulation described in Revelation chapters 6 through 19.

- The mid-tribulation view states Jesus will return at the *halfway point* of the seven-year tribulation. His return will coincide with Antichrist's invasion of the Jewish temple and the enforcement of the mark of the beast (Revelation 12–13).

- The post-tribulation view believes Christians will endure the entire tribulation and be rescued *just before* Christ returns at His second coming (Armageddon).

There is a fourth view, called the pre-wrath view, which sees the rapture taking place about five-and-a-half years into the tribulation. It is at this point, the proponents say, that the sixth seal is opened (Revelation 6:12) and God's wrath is poured out.

An obscure fifth view says that only certain believers will be taken in the rapture, while those who have been disobedient will be left behind to endure the tribulation. Very few serious Bible students believe in this partial-rapture perspective.

Three Views of the Millennium

As you might expect, there are also multiple interpretations about the nature of Jesus' millennial reign. Again, all of them hinge upon one's interpretive approach to Scripture (literal or symbolic).

Amillennialism—This view says the millennium is only a symbol of Christ's reign throughout the church age. Then at the end of the church age, He will return at His second coming. Typically, amillennialists must spiritualize the events of the tribulation to reach their conclusions. Some amillennialists are also preterists, believing that parts of the book of Revelation were fulfilled in the first century.

Postmillennialism—Those who hold this view must also spiritualize Revelation, seeing the church age as Christ's millennial reign. They believe the church will usher in the second coming of Christ by making the world more and more Christian. As it turns out, history and the moral and spiritual decline of the current age do not lend this view much credibility.

Premillennialism—Premillennialists see a literal 1,000-year reign of Christ upon the earth following the seven years of tribulation judgments. If you read Revelation at face value, no one could claim the seal, trumpet, and bowl judgments have happened at any point or time period in the last 2,000 years.

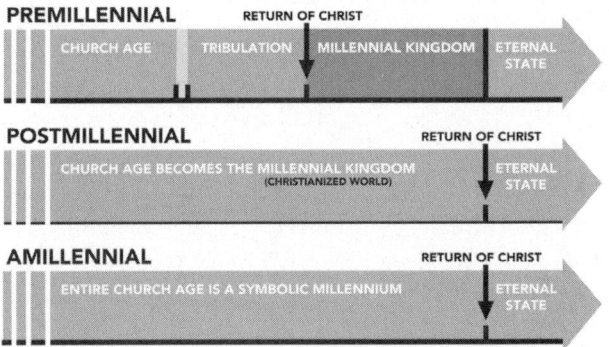

What We Can Agree on Even When We Disagree

So, which of these views is correct? Is it possible they all could have elements of truth to them? Does one have to be right over the others? Actually, yes, as each of these views mutually excludes the others (that is, Revelation's judgements cannot be both literal *and* figurative). So how do we as Christians handle the fact there are varying views about the end times among us?

First, it's okay for Christians to respectfully disagree when it comes to doctrines or teachings that don't touch upon the essentials of the faith—essentials such as the doctrines relating to our salvation. It's not required for us to have 100 percent uniformity on end-time issues in order to enjoy fellowship and experience unity in Christ.

Second, even literalists will admit there are still mysteries in certain areas of Bible prophecy. Not every prophetic detail about the future is spelled out for us in Daniel and Revelation. God hasn't revealed *all* the specifics to us in His Word. But that's been His pattern all along.[1] Admittedly, there are details that no one can know at this time.

Third, while there is room for disagreement, it is *not* okay for a Christian to remain in ignorance about the end times or to avoid a clear understanding of the various views. The apostle Paul was very passionate about Christians being informed, confident, and comforted regarding the truths of the last days (1 Thessalonians 4:13, 18; 2 Thessalonians 2:1-2, 5).

Fourth, it really does matter what you believe because your view of the end times will have a significant impact on your perspective, attitudes, and behavior right now (John 16:1-4). That is by God's prophetic design (Titus 2:13-15; 2 Peter 3:14; 1 John 3:2-3).

Chapter 9

HOW CAN BIBLE PROPHECY HELP CONVINCE SKEPTICS AND UNBELIEVERS?

One of the most challenging and intimidating responsibilities we face as Christians is defending our faith in a culture that is becoming increasingly more hostile toward Christianity and the Bible. We may sometimes feel outnumbered and outsmarted, and thus outmatched. It's not that we don't believe the truths of the Bible, but rather, that we struggle with defending those truths, especially to skeptics who have made up their minds about Jesus and His Word.

Today, there are many excellent apologetic resources (books, videos, and conferences) available to us, providing much-needed evidence and support for the faith using logic, philosophy, archaeology, and science. But what is sometimes left out is the apologetic of the Bible itself. This is unfortunate, because when it comes to solid evidence for Scripture's credibility, nothing is more compelling and convincing than fulfilled prophecy.

But before we jump into that together, let's address two important questions:

1. Why should I care about defending my faith?//
2. Why use prophecy to try and convince others of the Bible's reliability?

First, keep in mind that in Scripture, God calls every Christian to be an apologist, not just pastors and "professionals." All believers are called to "contend earnestly for the faith" (Jude 3). Peter also encourages us to put Jesus first, "always being ready to *make a defense* [give an answer] to everyone who asks you to give an account for the hope that is in you" (1 Peter 3:15). Peter uses the Greek word *apologia*, translated here as "make a defense." This word was used in the first century to describe an attorney presenting a reasonable, convincing case in a court of law.[1]

Second, we should use prophecy as an apologetic because it is one of the most concrete and undeniable proofs that God exists and that the Bible is true. On the day the church was born (Pentecost), Peter urged his fellow Jews to believe in Christ *because* of fulfilled Bible prophecy (Acts 2:14-16). Fulfilled prophecy was also used by the apostles in the early church to help convince some of the most skeptical unbelievers of their day (Acts 3:12-26; 13:13-41).

Another reason prophecy is so relevant and convincing is because of the fact we are seeing prophecies become fulfilled before our very eyes (see chapter 5).

Admittedly, none of us has the ability to convince an unwilling skeptic or a closed-minded unbeliever. Someone once said, "Even God can't steer a parked car." There must be at least some willingness on the part of a skeptic to consider the claims of Bible prophecy before being persuaded toward the truth. But the good news is that God delights in using His Word through people like us to lead others to salvation (2 Corinthians 5:11).

How Bible Prophecy Defends the Faith

Let's consider now some of the specific reasons Bible prophecy can be a powerful apologetic.

1. The Perfect Fulfillment of All the Prophecies That Have Come to Pass

The Bible is batting a thousand when it comes to fulfilled prophecy. It has never missed or been incorrect in the slightest manner, always hitting the bull's-eye exactly as God predicted. Every single prophecy concerning the Messiah's first coming was fulfilled literally and precisely as recorded in the Old Testament hundreds of years before Christ's birth. If even *one* of the Old Testament prophecies concerning Jesus' first coming turned out to be wrong, then we would have reason to question the Bible's authenticity. But this hasn't happened. On the contrary, because every one of these prophecies came true, we can expect all the prophecies concerning the end times and Jesus' second coming to also be fulfilled literally and precisely.

Fulfilled prophecy is strong evidence of the divine authorship of the Bible, for who but God could know the future and be able to predict it hundreds and thousands of years before it occurs? Jesus Himself declared that every single word of God will eventually be fulfilled, even down to the punctuation marks! (Matthew 5:17-18). Here are just a few of the more than 300 prophecies Jesus fulfilled at His first coming:

- He would be born to a virgin.[2]
- His physical place of birth was named.[3]
- He would ride into Jerusalem on a donkey.[4]
- He would be beaten and abused.[5]
- He would be betrayed with money.[6]
- His hands and feet would be pierced.[7]
- He would die with criminals.[8]
- His bones would not be broken on the cross.[9]
- Though killed with wicked men, His grave would be associated with a rich man.[10]
- He would physically rise from the dead.[11]

Now comes the math. The odds of one person fulfilling just *eight* of those prophecies is 1 in 1,000,000,000,000,000! Or one in one *quadrillion*.[12]

THE ODDS OF 1 PERSON FULFILLING JUST 8 PROPHECIES
1 IN 1 QUADRILLION
1,000,000,000,000,000

2. Credibility in the Area of Prophecy Is Evidence the Entire Bible Can Be Trusted

Because the Bible is accurate and credible when it comes to fulfilled prophecies, then it stands to reason that it can be trusted in other areas as well—science, history, morality, marriage and family, sexuality, relationships, and how to live (2 Timothy 3:16-17; 2 Peter 1:3-4).

3. Prophecy Is Being Fulfilled Before Our Very Eyes

We are currently witnessing many of Revelation's future prophecies in their embryonic forms. These are so blatantly obvious that they rise far above the category of mere coincidence. We touched on some of these in chapter 5. But let's take a closer look here.

The Bible makes it clear that before many of the events of Revelation can occur, the Jewish nation must be reborn and living in their ancient homeland (Jeremiah 30:1-51; Ezekiel 34:11-24; 37; Zechariah 10:6-10). This is the most-prophesied end-time event in the Bible, and it has *already happened*! Remember, the Jews were scattered to more than 100 nations for 20 centuries, where they were maligned, persecuted, and even slaughtered. And yet miraculously, through all that time, they retained their identity. Today, Israel is a nation once again, with more Jews living there than all other places in the world combined! Is that mere coincidence?

Both Daniel and Revelation, along with Jesus' Olivet Discourse in Matthew 24–25, tell us the Jews will also one day rebuild their temple in Jerusalem (Daniel 9:27; Matthew 24:15; 2 Thessalonians 2:3-4;

Revelation 11:1-2). The Temple Institute in Jerusalem was founded in 1987 with the express purpose of rebuilding that sacred structure on the Temple Mount. Those who are part of this institute have already fashioned sacred temple vessels and priestly garments according to Old Testament specifications. They have drawn up blueprints for the temple, trained priests, and even made preliminary sacrifices. At present, the institute is petitioning the Israeli government for permission to set foot on the Temple Mount itself to offer sacrifices in anticipation of the rebuilt temple. All they need is some sort of agreement or peace treaty enabling them to begin construction (Daniel 9:26-27). And according to Bible prophecy, that will happen with the simple stroke of a pen via an agreement signed by a world leader. Another mere coincidence?

Bible prophecy also tells us that in the last days a revived Roman Empire will rise up and function as a one-world government. Most recently, the coronavirus crisis prompted world leaders to say it's more urgent than ever to establish such a global governing entity. This teaches us that during a time of world crisis, the overwhelming consensus is going to be to "work together as one." The Bible indicates this will happen in a chaotic post-rapture world under the leadership of the man called Antichrist (Daniel 2:36-45; Revelation 13; 17:9-10). Do you think the Bible will just "get lucky" when this prophecy is fulfilled?

Scripture also predicts that when Jesus Christ returns at His second coming, His feet will touch the Mount of Olives, splitting it east to west, causing it to move north and south (Zechariah 14:4; Acts 1:11; Matthew 24:3). In 2004, NBC News reported that a three-year study by the Geological Survey of Israel confirmed this exact area to be at *imminent* risk for earthquakes, having detected a major fault line running—you guessed it—*right through the Mount of Olives*, east to west.[13] Just another coincidence? Or solid *evidence* that the Bible knows what it's talking about?

The Value of Bible Prophecy for Defending the Faith

The Bible has an established pattern of prophecies being fulfilled literally and accurately. For this reason, we can be absolutely certain the prophecies about Jesus' second coming, along with the hundreds of other end-time prophecies as of yet unfulfilled, are guaranteed to happen with 100 percent certainty. To deny this is to ignore the obvious and reliable track record of Scripture.

These are just some of the reasons Bible prophecy can serve as a powerful and effective apologetic. Of course, presenting these facts alone is not sufficient to change a person's mind and bring him or her to faith in Christ. For that to happen, we need the miraculous power of God and His Holy Spirit. It is His job to draw people to Jesus, to convict them of their sin and their desperate need for a Savior (John 6:44, 65; 16:7-11).

Peter wrote that in the end times, many will scoff at the prophecies concerning the last days (2 Peter 3:3-9). That highlights all the more the value of prophecy-related apologetics.

And now, more than ever.

Chapter 10

HOW SHOULD CHRISTIANS LIVE IF JESUS MIGHT RETURN ANY DAY NOW?

The reality of the rapture is a positive game-changer for our lives in many ways. But this is also where we may encounter some tension as well. For if Jesus really could come back today, should we still be going about our lives like we always do? Or should we instead focus only on the "spiritual stuff"?

The Protestant reformer Martin Luther is reported to have written, "Preach [and live] as if Jesus was crucified yesterday, rose from the dead today, and is returning tomorrow."

Good advice. But how does that counsel play out in our daily lives? How are we supposed to manage that spirit of expectancy while at the same time live life *normally*? Waiting for Christ to return does not mean we should sell all our possessions, climb the nearest mountain, and meditate until He returns. Nothing in the New Testament suggests we do this.

Contemplating the certainty of Jesus' coming should not guilt us into in sackcloth and ashes, ranting in the streets about judgment and the end of the world. The fact Christ's return is imminent doesn't mean we should become confrontational street preachers (this happens to be among the least effective evangelistic strategies for reaching our culture). How, then, should we respond to this prophetic truth?

A more sensible approach is for us to dig in and discover what the

Bible actually does tell us to do. Every New Testament author knew and believed that Jesus could return at any time to rescue His bride. And yet there is not even the slightest hint of panic or to suddenly begin a doomsday street-preaching ministry. What we do find is that Jesus, Paul, John, and Peter urge us to be faithful to the Lord, penetrate the darkness with light, and live a convincing life apologetic.

With that in mind, here are five guidelines that will help us toward this goal.

Perspective: Remembering This World Is Not My Home

As followers of Jesus, one of the paradoxes we live with is the fact that though we remain here on the earth right now, our citizenship is in heaven (Philippians 3:20). Our home is with the Lord. As Paul said, to remain here means we live for Christ, and to die is great gain (Galatians 2:20; Philippians 1:21). For Christians, this is a win-win proposition.

And though our time here on the earth is temporary, that certainly does not mean it's unimportant. The way we presently live will determine our future rewards in heaven (1 Corinthians 3:10-15; 2 Corinthians 5:10-11). So we maintain in our hearts and minds both an earthly and an eternal perspective. Our future influences our present. Knowing where we're going and who we'll be with should affect how we live in the here and now. Living with this perspective will give us great hope and encouragement.

Penetration: Shining the Light of Christ in a Dark World

It's no secret that we're living in evil days (Ephesians 5:16). Jesus' generation was no different, which is why He told His disciples,

> You are the light of the world. A city set on a hill cannot be hidden; nor does anyone light a lamp and put it under a basket, but on the lampstand, and it gives light to all who are in the house. Let your light shine before men in such a way that they may see your good works, and glorify your Father who is in heaven (Matthew 5:14-16).

If Jesus wanted His bride to be in heaven right now, that's exactly where she would be. And even though we are in the last days, we still do not know how long we will be here. We could live out our entire lifetime, or we could be called home tomorrow. But no matter how long we will remain here on earth, we must shine His light for the duration.

The tendency of many Christians is to think that only activities like Bible study, prayer, and church are truly spiritual in nature. But the truth is that the most spiritual thing we can do is to simply be obedient and faithful to God in the daily tasks He has called us to right now. That means being a faithful student, employee, boss, husband, wife, mother, father, son, daughter, or whatever role He has placed you in at this time. Jesus would never ask you to abandon the responsibilities that come with your everyday role in order to focus solely upon His return.

Preparation: Making Myself Ready to Meet the Lord

John wrote, "Beloved, now we are children of God, and it has not appeared as yet what we will be. We know that when He appears, we will be like Him, because we will see Him just as He is. And everyone who has this hope fixed on Him purifies himself, just as He is pure" (1 John 3:2-3). A bride's greatest desire is to be ready and prepared for her wedding day and her husband.

Writing about Jesus' return and the ultimate destruction of the earth, the apostle Peter concluded,

> Since all these things are to be destroyed in this way, what sort of people ought you to be in holy conduct and godliness, looking for and hastening the coming of the day of God, because of which the heavens will be destroyed by burning, and the elements will melt with intense heat! But according to His promise we are looking for new heavens and a new earth, in which righteousness dwells (2 Peter 3:11-13).

In those few verses, Peter gives us a healthy balance between living purely and watching for the day of the Lord. Knowing that Christ could return at any time not only motivates us to be holy in our conduct, but also fills us with expectant hope while we live!

When my (Jeff) wife was pregnant with our first son, we spent almost nine months of waiting, preparing, and looking forward to that day when he would finally arrive. But during that extended period of time, I continued to go to work, take care of the house, spend time with my wife, and meet with friends. And yet every day I kept reminding myself that soon I would be a father. It was that future reality that caused me to want to be the best I could be as a pastor, husband, and dad.

Christ's promised return does the same thing for us as believers. It puts purpose and passion into our daily lives, motivating and preparing us to meet Him.

Priorities: God Must Remain Number One in My Life

Have you ever secretly prayed, "Jesus, I want You to return, but could You just hold off Your coming until I can get married?...finish college?...get my graduate degree?...have children?...see my kids grow up?" These are natural desires and we shouldn't think of them as inherently selfish. They're all a part of living our lives here on earth. Such desires become a problem only when we care about them *more* than we do about God Himself. Jesus made it clear that our love for Him must far outweigh our love for anyone or anything else, including ourselves (Luke 14:25-35). When we love the world and the things of the world more than the things of God, we will slide into spiritual mediocrity and become lukewarm (James 4:4; 1 John 2:15-17; Revelation 3:14-16). But as long as God truly remains our number one priority, we can freely pursue all these other lesser desires in the right ways.

When we delight ourselves in the Lord, He puts in our hearts the desires He wants us to have (Psalm 37:4). No guilt. Only gratitude that we are free to love Him and live our lives to the fullest while, at the same time, longing for our Savior's return.

ENDNOTES

Chapter 1—What Is Bible Prophecy, and Why Is It Such a Big Deal?
1. Isaiah 46:9-11.
2. See, for example, the prophecies and fulfillments in Micah 5:2 and Matthew 2:1-6; Isaiah 7:14 and Matthew 1:21-23; Daniel 9:24-25 and Luke 19:37-42; Zechariah 9:9 and Matthew 21:4-5; Zechariah 11:12 and Matthew 26:14-15; Psalm 22:18 and Matthew 27:35; Psalm 22:1 and Matthew 27:46; Isaiah 53:12 and Mark 14:27-28.
3. See, for example:

   Romans 13:11—"knowing the *time* [Greek, *kairos*—era, age], that it is *already* the hour"

   Romans 13:12—"The night is almost gone, and the day is *near*."

   1 Corinthians 1:7—"*awaiting eagerly* the revelation of our Lord Jesus Christ"

   1 Corinthians 16:22—"*Maranatha*" (used by the early Church for hello or goodbye, from an Aramaic expression meaning "our Lord, come").

   Philippians 3:20—"heaven, from which we also *eagerly wait* for a Savior"

   Philippians 4:5—"The Lord is *near*."

   1 Thessalonians 1:10—"to *wait* for His Son from heaven"

   Titus 2:13—"…*looking for blessed hope* and the *appearing* of…Christ Jesus."

   James 5:7-8—"Be patient, therefore brethren, until the *coming of the Lord*…be patient; strengthen your hearts, for the coming of the Lord is *near*."

   Hebrews 9:28—"Christ…shall *appear a second time* for salvation without reference to sin, *to those who eagerly await Him*."

   Hebrews 10:25—"…encouraging one another; and all the more *as you see the day drawing near*."

   Hebrews 10:37—"For yet *in a very little while*, He who is coming *will come*, and will *not delay*."

   1 Peter 1:13—"*Fix your hope* completely on the grace to be brought to you at the revelation of Jesus Christ."

   1 Peter 4:7—"The end of all things is *near*."

   1 John 2:18—"we *know* that this is the *last hour*"

   Jude 21—"*waiting anxiously* for the mercy of our Lord Jesus Christ"

   Revelation 3:11—"*I am coming quickly*; hold fast what you have."

   Revelation 22:7—"Behold, *I am coming quickly*."

   Revelation 22:12—"Behold, *I am coming quickly*."

   Revelation 22:20—"Yes, *I am coming quickly*."

Chapter 2—In What Basic Order Will the End Times Unfold?
1. Times of Israel staff, "Israel ranked world's 8th most powerful country; no longer in Top 10 'movers,'" *The Times of Israel*, March 5, 2019, https://www.timesofisrael.com/israel-ranked-8th-most-powerful-country-in-the-world/.

QUICK REFERENCE GUIDE TO THE END TIMES

Chapter 3—How Do We Know Jesus Is Literally Returning to Earth?

1. Preterists appeal to Jesus' words in Matthew 24:34 as evidence of their view that "this generation shall not pass away until all these things take place."

2. Preterists also believe John wrote Revelation prior to AD 70, not in AD 95. Obviously, if Revelation were written around AD 90, then their interpretation of the events of AD 70 would not have been prophetic because they had already occurred. But again, no one ever documented such events or judgments as having taken place. Among the evidences for a later (AD 95) date is the belief of the early church fathers, including Irenaeus (AD 180), whose teacher (Polycarp) was a direct disciple of John. This same Polycarp also in AD 110 wrote that the church at Smyrna didn't even exist in AD 65. The church at Laodicea was still recovering from a mighty earthquake that took place in AD 60, and it took about 25 years to rebuild the city. The church hardly would have been described as "rich, wealthy, and in need of nothing" by Jesus at that time (Revelation 3:17).

3. **Secular sources** include Josephus, Tacitus, Pliny The Younger, Lucian, Phelgon, Celus, Mara Bar Serapion, Suetonius, and Thallus. **New Testament sources** include Matthew, Mark, Luke, John, Paul, the author of Hebrews, James, Peter, and Jude. **Nonbiblical Christian sources** include Clement of Rome, 2 Clement, Ignatius, Polycarp, Martyrdom of Polycarp, Didache, Barnabas, Shepherd of Hermas, Fragments of Papias, Justin Martyr, Aristides, Athenagoras, Theophilus of Antioch, Quadratus, Aristo of Pella, Melito of Sardis, Diognetus, Gospel of Peter, Apocalypse of Peter, and Epistula Apostolorum. From apologist Frank Turek at https://crossexamined.org/did-jesus-exist/.

4. See also Matthew 24:30.

5. This spirit of expectancy is evident in the following verses:

    Romans 13:11—"knowing the time, that it is already the hour"

    Romans 13:12—"The night is almost gone, and the day is near."

    1 Corinthians 1:7—"awaiting eagerly the revelation of our Lord Jesus Christ"

    1 Corinthians 16:22—"Maranatha" (used by the early church for hello or goodbye, from an Aramaic expression meaning "our Lord, come").

    Philippians 3:20—"For our citizenship is in heaven, from which also we eagerly wait for a Savior."

    Philippians 4:5—"The Lord is near."

    1 Thessalonians 1:10—"to wait for His Son from heaven"

    Titus 2:13—"…looking for the blessed hope and the appearing of the glory of our great God and Savior, Christ Jesus."

    James 5:7-8—"Therefore be patient, brethren, until the coming of the Lord…be patient; strengthen your hearts, for the coming of the Lord is near."

    Hebrews 9:28—"Christ also…will appear a second time for salvation without reference to sin, to those who eagerly await Him."

    Hebrews 10:25—"…encouraging one another; and all the more as you see the day drawing near."

    Hebrews 10:37—"For yet in a very little while, He who is coming will come, and will not delay."

Endnotes

1 Peter 1:13—"Fix your hope completely on the grace to be brought to you at the revelation of Jesus Christ."

1 Peter 4:7—"The end of all things is near."

1 John 2:18—"we know that it is the last hour"

Jude 21—"waiting anxiously for the mercy of our Lord Jesus Christ"

Revelation 3:11—"I am coming quickly; hold fast what you have."

Revelation 22:7—"Behold, I am coming quickly."

Revelation 22:12—"Behold, I am coming quickly."

Revelation 22:20—"Yes, I am coming quickly."

Excerpted from Jeff Kinley, *Wake the Bride* (Eugene, OR: Harvest House, 2015), 77-79.

Chapter 4—What Is the Rapture, and Who Will Be Taken?

1. Strong's Concordance #726, *harpazó*, https://biblehub.com.
2. "Pastors: The End of the World Is Complicated," *LifeWay Research*, April 26, 2016, https://lifewayresearch.com/2016/04/26/pastors-the-end-of-the-world-is-complicated/.

Chapter 8—What Are the Different Views of the End Times, and Why Does It Matter?

1. God told Micah the Messiah would be born in Bethlehem, but He did not pinpoint the exact house or time (Micah 5:2). The Lord told Isaiah the Messiah would be born of a virgin, but He didn't tell him which virgin, how old she would be, or that she would already be betrothed at the time of her conception (Isaiah 7:14). Scripture gives us a detailed composite sketch of Antichrist's character and actions, but it does not tell us his identity or name.

Chapter 9—How Can Bible Prophecy Help Convince Skeptics and Unbelievers?

1. Acts 22:1; 25:16; 1 Corinthians 9:3; Philippians 1:7, 16; 1 Peter 3:15.
2. Genesis 3:15; Galatians 4:4; Isaiah 7:14; Matthew 1:22-23.
3. Micah 5:2; Matthew 2:5-6; Luke 2:4-6.
4. Zechariah 9:9; Matthew 21:4-5.
5. Isaiah 50:6; Matthew 26:67; 27:26.
6. Zechariah 11:12-13; Matthew 27:9-10.
7. Psalms 22:16; Zechariah 12:10; John 19:34, 37.
8. Isaiah 53:12; Matthew 27:38.
9. Psalm 34:20; John 19:33-36.
10. Isaiah 53:9; Matthew 27:57-60.
11. Psalms 16:10; Matthew 28:2-7.
12. Peter Stoner, *Science Speaks* (Chicago: Moody Press, 1969), 106-7.
13. See at http://discussions.godandscience.org/viewtopic.php?t=38866.

PROPHECY PROS

Two experts. One topic. No confusion.

Jeff and Todd are on a mission to reach the next generation with the inspiring, hopeful message found in Bible prophecy through books, events, and other resources such as:

PROPHECY PROS PODCAST

THE DANIEL PROJECT
LIVE EVENTS

Jeff Kinley

Jeff Kinley is a best-selling author of more than 30 books and speaks all across America, motivating Christians to live for Christ and to prepare for His soon coming. His weekly VintageTruth Podcast is heard in over 80 countries.
Learn more at JeffKinley.com

Todd Hampson

Todd Hampson is a best-selling author, illustrator, and animation producer. His Non-Prophet's Guide™ book series has opened up the world of Bible prophecy and eschatology to a new generation of truth-seekers.
Learn more at ToddHampson.com

FOR MORE INFORMATION, VISIT:
PROPHECYPROSPODCAST.COM | THEPROPHECYPROS.COM